My Friend
JESUS

By REV. LAWRENCE G. LOVASIK, S.V.D.
Divine Word Missionary

CATHOLIC BOOK PUBLISHING CO.
NEW YORK, N. Y.

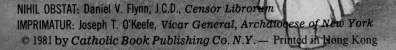

NIHIL OBSTAT: Daniel V. Flynn, J.C.D., *Censor Librorum*
IMPRIMATUR: Joseph T. O'Keefe, *Vicar General, Archdiocese of New York*
© 1981 by *Catholic Book Publishing Co. N.Y.* — Printed in Hong Kong

Jesus Became a Child Like Me

JESUS, my Friend,
   for love of me,
   You were born
   of the Virgin Mary,
   and became a child like me.

You wanted to work and suffer,
   and even to die on the Cross,
   to show Your love for me,
   and to save my soul.

I give myself to You,
   with all the love of my heart,
   in the arms of Your sweet Mother,
   and will never leave Your Heart.

Jesus Lived in a Family

JESUS, my Friend,
    when still a little boy,
    You loved and obeyed
    Your dearest Mother Mary
    and good Saint Joseph.

You helped them in their work,
    because this was Your Father's will.

Teach me to love my parents,
    to obey them for Your sake,
    and to help them every way I can.

I want to do this
    to let You know I love You
    and want to be like You.
    I want to make them happy
    because they take Your place.

Jesus Gave Me His Family

JESUS, Mary, and Joseph,
  I ask for your help
    that I may live a good life.

Jesus, Mary, and Joseph,
  I give you my heart
  and my soul.

Jesus, Mary, and Joseph,
  help me
  when I am dying.

Jesus, Mary, and Joseph,
  may I die in peace
  with you.

Jesus Is My Shepherd

JESUS, my Friend,
    You are my Good Shepherd.
    You care for my soul,
    and lead me in ways of peace.

Make me a good sheep.
    Let me listen to Your voice,
    and ever follow You
    till I reach You in heaven.

If I stray into ways of sin,
    lead me back again
    to Your loving Heart.

Keep me in Your gentle arms,
    dearest Shepherd of my soul,
    till You see Your little sheep
    safe in heaven's fold.

Jesus Is My Teacher

JESUS, my Friend,
  You came from heaven
  to teach me to be
  pure and kind and good
  as You are.

I want to be like You,
    and please You in all I do.

Give me Your grace to help me
    to live as You lived,
    and to keep from every sin.

I give You my heart in truest love
    and want to serve You faithfully,
    because You have done so much
      for me,
    and gave Your Heart to me.

Jesus Helps Me to Learn

JESUS, my Friend,
   I offer You
   my thoughts, words, and deeds,
   and every pain I feel.

I offer You my work in school,
   and all my fun and play.

l want to study hard for You,
   because this is what You want.

Send me Your Holy Spirit
   to give me light and help
   in all my studies,
   above all, in my Catechism.

I want You to be
   my best Friend.
   Take me to heaven some day.

Jesus Died for Me

JESUS, my Friend,
    I thank You for all You have done
    to show Your love for me:

You became a Child,
    and died on the Cross for me.

Now You give Yourself to me
    in Holy Communion
    and fill my heart with grace.

I give You my heart
    because You gave me Yours.

I beg You to forgive me
    for the many times
    I hurt Your loving Heart,
    and did not act
    like a friend of Yours.

Jesus Forgives My Sins

JESUS, my Friend and my God,
    I am sorry for all my sins
    because they have offended You.

You died on the Cross
    because of my sins.

I want to try hard
        to keep away from sin,
        so that I may always be Your friend
        and show You that I really love You.

I pray for the many sinners
        who do not know Your love.

Forgive them as You did on the Cross.
        Give them true sorrow for their sins
        and lead them to Your Sacred Heart.

Jesus Comes to Me in Communion

JESUS, my Friend,
You give Yourself to me
as Food in Holy Communion.
You offer Yourself for me
in every Holy Mass
as You did upon the Cross.

I adore You as my God
in the Sacrament of the Altar
where Your Heart is all on fire
with deepest love for me.

Jesus Gives Me Friends

JESUS, my Friend,
   when I am sick I offer my pain to You
   because You suffered on the Cross for me.

Thank You for the friends who come to visit me
   and for those who take care of me.

You are my best Friend when I need help.
   I know You will never leave me.

Jesus Gave Me My Family

JESUS, my Friend,
   bless my mother and my father
   for all they do for me.

Give them grace and health
   now on earth.

Then in heaven
   give them a great reward —
   give them Your own dear Self.

Give our family peace and love,
   so that we may have a happy home.
   Help us to do Your will
   and meet in heaven again.

Jesus Gave Me a Guardian Angel

JESUS, my Friend,
  I thank You
    for giving me an Angel,
    who is ever at my side
    to help me to be good,
    and to keep me from harm.

I want to listen to my Angel's voice
        because I know
        that what my Angel tells me
        is what You want me to do.

With my Angel's help
      I will always try
      to love You more,
      and never hurt You by sin.

As my Angel is my friend on earth,
      may he be my friend in heaven,
      where we both can love You
      forever.

24

Jesus Gave Me His Mother

JESUS, my Friend,
  I thank You for giving me
  Your loving Mother Mary
  to be my Mother, too.

Keep me safe in her loving care
    that I may never hurt You by sin,
    or ever forget Your love for me.

Hear Your Mother's prayers for me.
    Make my body pure
    and my soul holy.
    Give me all the grace I need
    ever to be Your friend.

VIRGIN Mary,
  You are my Mother.
Keep me safe, that I may never
    hurt Your Son by sin.
Help me to please Him always.

Jesus Listens to Those Who Love Mary

JESUS, my Friend,
by all the love You feel
in Your Heart for Mary,
by all her love for You,
make me love her more.

Let her fill my heart
with greater love for You.

And when I have to die,
remember, Lord, I love Your Mother.

Through her prayers I hope
You will forgive my sins,
and take me to Your Heart.

Jesus, My Best Friend

JESUS, You came on earth
to be our Best Friend
and teach us how to live
in order to please You and the Father.

Help me to be close to You,
to avoid sin and do good.
Keep me ever in Your grace
and in close union with You.

I want to make You my Best Friend
for my whole life.
My Lord and my God,
I love You with my whole heart.

Jesus Loves All Children

JESUS, my Friend,
  You are the Friend of children.
  Bless the children
  of the whole world.

Never let us forget
  that You are our best Friend
  Who died on the Cross for us.

Your gave Your love to us;
  may we give our love to You.

Keep us ever very close
  to Your loving Heart,
  that we may always be
  pure and kind,
  and obedient to Your Will.

Lead us all to heaven some day,
  where we can love and thank You,
  with Your dearest Mother Mary,
  in joys that never end.

Jesus — My Friend in the Eucharist

JESUS, my Friend, You promised
    to be with us till the end of time.
    in the Sacrament of the Altar.

Give me the Bread from heaven
    that I may have eternal life
    in the Kingdom You prepared for me.